GIANNIS
ANTETOKOUNMPO

SARAH MACHAJEWSKI

PowerKiDS press.

New York

Published in 2019 by The Rosen Publishing Group, Inc.
29 East 21st Street, New York, NY 10010

First Edition

Editor: Elizabeth Krajnik
Book Design: Michael Flynn

Photo Credits: Cover, p. 1 Vaughn Ridley/Getty Images Sport/Getty Images; cover, pp. 4–6, 8–16, 18, 21–23 (background) Eo naya/Shutterstock.com; p. 5 Ververidis Vasilis/Shutterstock.com; p. 6 Cherdchai charasri/Shutterstock.com; p. 7 Jamie McCarthy/Getty Images Entertainment/Getty Images; p. 9 Ronald Martinez/Getty Images Sport/Getty Images; p. 10 Pacific Press/LightRocket/Getty Images; p. 11 NurPhoto/Getty Images; p. 13 Elsa/Getty Images Sport/Getty Images; p. 15 Mike Strobe/Getty Images Sport/Getty Images; p. 17 Jared Wickerham/Getty Images Sport/Getty Images; p. 19 Sacramento Bee/Tribune News Service/Getty Images; p. 21 Mike McGinnis/Getty Images Sport/Getty Images; p. 22 Dylan Buell/Getty Images Sport/Getty Images.

Library of Congress Cataloging-in-Publication Data

Names: Machajewski, Sarah, author.
Title: Giannis Antetokounmpo / Sarah Machajewski.
Description: New York : PowerKids Press, [2019] | Series: Young sports greats
  | Includes index.
Identifiers: LCCN 2018014062| ISBN 9781538330432 (library bound) | ISBN
  9781538330456 (paperback) | ISBN 9781538330463 (6 pack)
Subjects: LCSH: Antetokounmpo, Giannis, 1994–Juvenile literature. |
  Basketball players–United States–Biography–Juvenile literature. |
  Milwaukee Bucks (Basketball team)–History–Juvenile literature.
Classification: LCC GV884.A56 M33 2019 | DDC 796.323092 [B] –dc23
LC record available at https://lccn.loc.gov/2018014062

Manufactured in the United States of America

CPSIA Compliance Information: Batch #CS18PK For Further Information contact Rosen Publishing, New York, New York at 1-800-237-9932

CONTENTS

MEET GIANNIS

In the fast-paced game of basketball, height and skill are pretty important. Rising basketball star Giannis Antetokounmpo doesn't have to worry about either of those things. Standing at a towering six feet 11 inches (210.8 cm) tall, Antetokounmpo turns heads not just for his height, but also for his talent.

Today, Antetokounmpo is a famous National Basketball Association (NBA) **small forward** for the Milwaukee Bucks. However, he started as a beginner just like all other **professional** athletes. Through hard work and **determination**, Antetokounmpo caught the eye of some of the best teams in the United States. Since being **drafted** by the Bucks, Antetokounmpo has quickly risen to fame and greatness.

SPORTS CORNER

Basketball was invented in 1891. A man named James Naismith thought up an indoor game that was meant to be easy yet interesting, and it was an instant success—and has been ever since.

ANTETOKOUNMPO SLAM-DUNKS THE BALL AT THE ANTETOKOUNBROS STREETBALL EVENT IN THESSALONIKI, GREECE, ON MAY 22, 2016.

HARD TIMES IN GREECE

Antetokounmpo was born near Athens, Greece, on December 6, 1994. His parents **immigrated** to Greece from Nigeria in 1991, leaving behind their oldest son, Francis, with his grandparents. Even though Antetokounmpo was born in Greece, he didn't receive full Greek **citizenship** until he was 18 years old.

Antetokounmpo's early life wasn't easy. When he was younger, his mother was sick and his father struggled to find work. Poor and often hungry, Antetokounmpo and his brother, Thanasis, sold small **trinkets** such as sunglasses and toys on the streets in Greece. They used the money they made to help their family pay their bills and buy groceries.

ATHANASIOS, OR THANASIS, ANTETOKOUNMPO (PICTURED LEFT) IS ALSO A SMALL FORWARD AND PLAYS FOR PANATHINAIKOS, A GREEK PROFESSIONAL BASKETBALL TEAM.

A NATURAL ATHLETE

Antetokounmpo and his brothers were encouraged to try basketball by a coach named Spiros Velliniatis. Antetokounmpo picked up a basketball for the first time ever in 2007, when he was 13 years old. No one could've known that it would change his life forever.

Antetokounmpo played basketball for Filathlitikos, a basketball club in a neighborhood outside Athens. However, sometimes he had to miss practice so he could help his family. Antetokounmpo's club and coaches helped his parents find work and helped the family with money and food. Soon, Antetokounmpo began to get stronger and healthier—and that's when he started showing real talent on the court.

SPORTS CORNER

Basketball talent runs in the Antetokounmpo family. Giannis's brother Thanasis played for the New York Knicks in 2016 and now plays for Greece's national team. His younger brothers show a talent for the sport, too.

ANTETOKOUNMPO DEMONSTRATED ATHLETIC TALENT FROM AN EARLY AGE. HE WON MEDALS IN DIFFERENT SPORTS HE PLAYED AT SCHOOL. HE'S COME A LONG WAY SINCE THEN!

YOUNG AND TALENTED

On the Filathlitikos youth team—one of Greece's best—Antetokounmpo stood out on the court in the position of point guard. After seeing him play, a **scout** once said, "Guys who are 6'9" with that kind of skill set, especially at that age…there's not many [of them]."

ANTETOKOUNMPO HELPED THE GREEK TEAM IN THE 2016 INTERNATIONAL BASKETBALL FEDERATION (FIBA) OLYMPIC QUALIFYING **TOURNAMENT** AGAINST THE IRANIAN TEAM IN TURIN, ITALY.

In 2012, Antetokounmpo moved up to the Filathlitikos senior team. During the 2012–2013 season, he played for them in the Greek A2 League. He played 26 games, averaging 9.5 points per game, 5 **rebounds**, 1.4 **assists**, and made 62.1 percent of the shots he took.

ATTRACTING ATTENTION

The 2012–2013 basketball season was a great one for Antetokounmpo. In just five short years, he had transformed, or changed, from an unknown player into Greece's top basketball talent. Scouts throughout Greece had their eyes on him.

Antetokounmpo was **recruited** to Greece's Under 20 basketball team and played in the 2013 U20 European Championships. Over 10 tournament games, Antetokounmpo averaged 8 points per game, 7.6 rebounds, and 2.2 assists. He also played in the Greek League All-Star Games, where he reached career highs of 23 points per game, 10 rebounds, and 4 blocks. These impressive stats attracted the attention of scouts all over the world.

SPORTS CORNER

Just days after Antetokounmpo turned 18 years old, he signed a four-year contract with the Spanish club CAI Zaragoza. Other teams, including FC Barcelona Bàsquet and Anadolu Efes, were interested in signing him.

THE SAME YEAR ANTETOKOUNMPO SIGNED A CONTRACT WITH CAI ZARAGOZA, HE ALSO SIGNED A FOUR-YEAR DEAL WITH NIKE. MANY ATHLETES DREAM OF A MOMENT LIKE THIS!

GOING PRO

Soon, people from the NBA began hearing about a promising young player from Greece. Scouts from all over the league traveled to see Antetokounmpo in action, but he was still an unknown player with raw talent. His chances of getting into the NBA depended on a team believing in his potential, or ability to become successful.

In the end, the Milwaukee Bucks chose Antetokounmpo as the 15th overall pick in the first round of the 2013 NBA draft. The team gained a player with promise and a huge **wingspan**. Antetokounmpo signed his first NBA contract in July 2013. He was just 19 years old!

SPORTS CORNER

Antetokounmpo's four-year contract with CAI Zaragoza included an NBA buyout. That means if an NBA team wanted him, Antetokounmpo could break his contract with CAI Zaragoza to play on the NBA team.

THE 2013 NBA DRAFT CHANGED ANTETOKOUNMPO'S
LIFE FOREVER.

Antetokounmpo made his NBA debut, or first appearance, wearing number 34 for the Milwaukee Bucks in the 2013–2014 season. Playing the position of forward, he appeared in 77 games during his rookie, or first, year.

Over the course of the season, Antetokounmpo put up double-digit points 23 times, grabbed rebounds, successfully blocked his opponents, and pulled off a few **double-doubles**. He earned a spot on the 2013–2014 NBA All-Rookie Team and an appearance in the NBA All-Star Weekend. At the end of the season, Antetokounmpo was a leading rookie in the NBA.

ANTETOKOUNMPO'S ROOKIE STATS					
GAMES PLAYED	AVERAGE POINTS	AVERAGE REBOUNDS	AVERAGE ASSISTS	AVERAGE STEALS	AVERAGE BLOCKS
77	6.8	4.4	1.9	0.8	0.8

ANTETOKOUNMPO'S ROOKIE STATS MADE HIM ONE OF THE MOST PROMISING YOUNG PLAYERS IN THE NBA.

"THE GREEK FREAK"

There was no doubt that Antetokounmpo was a good player, but he needed time to get better. He once said, "I don't want to be a good player. I want to be a great player." Throughout his second and third season, he improved greatly. His stats grew stronger each year. In the 2016–2017 season, Antetokounmpo scored an average of 22.9 points per game.

Antetokounmpo's fan base grew along with him. His incredible talent for basketball and his nationality earned him the nickname "The Greek Freak." After the 2016–2017 season, Antetokounmpo was named an NBA All Star and won that year's Most Improved Player award.

OVER THE LAST FIVE YEARS, ALL ELEMENTS OF ANTETOKOUNMPO'S GAME HAVE IMPROVED, FROM HIS AVERAGE NUMBER OF POINTS SCORED TO FIELD GOALS AND MORE.

ANTETOKOUNMPO'S STATS 2013–2018

YEAR	AVERAGE POINTS	FIELD GOAL %	FREE THROW %	AVERAGE STEALS	AVERAGE BLOCKS
2017–18	29.8	54.4	76.6	1.9	1.5
2016–17	22.9	52.1	77.0	1.6	1.9
2015–16	16.9	50.6	72.4	1.2	1.4
2014–15	12.7	49.1	74.1	0.9	1.0
2013–14	6.8	41.4	68.3	0.8	0.8

ALREADY ONE OF THE GREATS

The Milwaukee Bucks see how great of a player they have in Antetokounmpo. Historically, the Bucks have struggled to compete with better teams in bigger cities. However, Antetokounmpo is helping turn that around. In 2016, the team signed him to a four-year, $100 million contract.

With the Bucks, Antetokounmpo hopes to continue improving and earn the NBA's Most Valuable Player award. He's bulked up to 235 pounds (106.6 kg), and is getting stronger and better every year. Already, experts and fans are comparing Antetokounmpo to basketball greats like Kevin Durant, Kobe Bryant, and Steph Curry. And he's just 23 years old!

SPORTS CORNER

Antetokounmpo ended the 2016–2017 season as a top 20 NBA player in total points, rebounds, assists, steals, and blocks.

KOBE BRYANT CHALLENGED ANTETOKOUNMPO TO WIN THE 2016–2017 MVP TITLE.

A BRIGHT FUTURE

Giannis Antetokounmpo began his life as an athlete as a young, unknown player on a youth basketball team in Greece. Now one of the NBA's most famous faces, Antetokounmpo has come a long way from his tough childhood. His dreams of escaping a life of being poor have come true—and it's only going to get better from here.

Antetokounmpo's future in professional basketball is bright. His most recent season already looks better than the last, and basketball fans everywhere are sure to keep their eyes on this young rising star.

GLOSSARY

assist: The act of a player who helps a teammate score a goal.

citizenship: The state of being a citizen, or someone who legally belongs to a country and has the rights and protection of that country.

determination: A quality that makes a person continue trying to do or achieve something difficult.

double-double: In basketball, when a player reaches double-digit points in two statistical categories.

draft: To choose someone to play on a professional sports team, and also the event during which this happens.

immigrate: To come to a country to live there.

professional: Having to do with a job someone does for a living.

rebound: In basketball, the recovery of the ball after a missed shot.

recruit: To persuade a person to join a sports team.

scout: A person whose job it is to search for talented athletes.

small forward: A basketball forward who is usually smaller than a power forward and whose play is characterized by quickness and scoring ability.

tournament: A series of contests played to see which team is the best and to win a prize.

trinket: A small object of little value.

wingspan: The distance from the tip of the hand to the tip of the other hand when a person's arms are outstretched.

INDEX

WEBSITES

Due to the changing nature of Internet links, PowerKids Press has developed an online list of websites related to the subject of this book. This site is updated regularly. Please use this link to access the list: www.powerkidslinks.com/ysg/giannis